Buzz, Hop, Zip!

Written by Samantha Montgomerie

Collins

This bug is quick.

six legs

This bug sings.

It hums songs.

This bug rubs its wings.

buzz

This bug hops.

Its long legs push.

This bug is in a web.

buzz

10

This bug has wings.

It zips off!

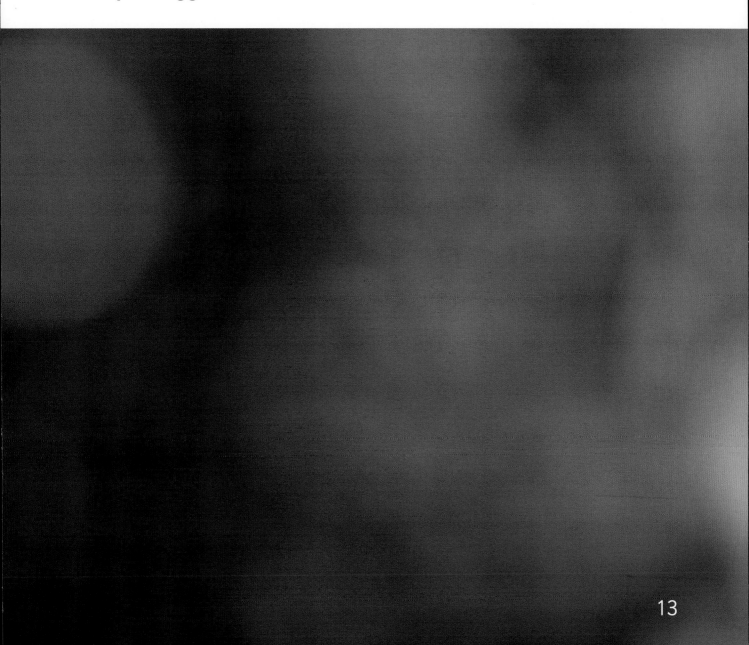

/qu/

14

After reading

Letters and Sounds: Phase 3

Word count: 39

Focus phonemes: /w/ /x/ /z/ /qu/ /th/ /ng/ , zz

Common exception words: and, push

Curriculum links: Understanding the World

Early learning goals: Reading: read and understand simple sentences; use phonic knowledge to decode regular words and read them aloud accurately; read some common irregular words

Developing fluency

- Your child may enjoy hearing you read the book.
- Take turns to read a page with your child. Ensure they also read the labels and sound words. On page 13, demonstrate how to read the sentence as an exclamation, using a tone of surprise.

Phonic practice

- Focus on words with the /ng/ sound and challenge your child to sound out and blend the following:

  sings   songs   wings   rings   pings   bongs   dongs   things

- Turn to page 2. Point to **quick** and challenge your child to sound out and blend. Can they identify the two pairs of letters that each make one sound? (/qu/, /ck/)
- Look at the "I spy sounds" on pages 14–15 together. Ask your child to describe what they can see. Next, take turns to find a word in the picture containing a /qu/, /z/ or zz sound. (e.g. *queen, squirrel, zipper, buzz*)

Extending vocabulary

- Look at pages 8–9. Ask your child to explain what the bug is doing.
  - Ask your child to point to and read the word that shows what the bug does. (*hops*)
  - Ask your child to point to and read the word that shows what its legs do. (*push*)
  - Can your child think of synonyms (similar words) for **hops**? (e.g. *jumps, springs*)